PAINTING PROVERBS

TEMPHEST BLUE

authorHOUSE®

AuthorHouse™
1663 Liberty Drive
Bloomington, IN 47403
www.authorhouse.com
Phone: 1 (800) 839-8640

Published by AuthorHouse 06/12/2017

ISBN: 978-1-5246-9635-1 (sc)
ISBN: 978-1-5246-9634-4 (e)

Print information available on the last page.

Any people depicted in stock imagery provided by Thinkstock are models, and such images are being used for illustrative purposes only.
Certain stock imagery © Thinkstock.

This book is printed on acid-free paper.

Because of the dynamic nature of the Internet, any web addresses or links contained in this book may have changed since publication and may no longer be valid. The views expressed in this work are solely those of the author and do not necessarily reflect the views of the publisher, and the publisher hereby disclaims any responsibility for them.

Scripture quotations marked KJV are from the Holy Bible, King James Version (Authorized Version). First published in 1611. Quoted from the KJV Classic Reference Bible, Copyright © 1983 by The Zondervan Corporation.

I PURPOSELY SOLD YOU ALL MY AMBITIONS, IDEAS, AND

DREAMS BECAUSE I KNEW YOU WOULD BELIEVE IN THEM SO

MUCH THAT WHEN I BEGAN TO DOUBT MYSELF YOU WOULD SELL THEM BACK TO ME...

BUT NEVER AT THE PRICE OF "I TOLD YOU SO"

THAT'S WHY I LOVED YOU SO.

THANK YOU MOM

PROVERBS 1:7(a) The fear of the LORD
is the beginning of knowledge:

Please Illustrate or draw your own interpretation of the Scripture:

**PROVERBS 1:7(a) The fear of the LORD
is the beginning of knowledge:**

PROVEBS 2:22 But the wicked shall
be cut off from the earth, and the
transgressors shall be rooted out of it.

Please Illustrate or draw your own interpretation of the Scripture:

PROVEBS 2:22 But the wicked shall
be cut off from the earth, and the
transgressors shall be rooted out of it.

PROVERBS 3:1 My son, forget not my law; but let thine heart keep my commandments:

Please Illustrate or draw your own interpretation of the Scripture:

**PROVERBS 3:1 My son, forget not my law; but
let thine heart keep my commandments:**

PROVERBS 4:8 Exalt her, and she shall promote thee: she shall bring thee to honour, when thou dost embrace her.

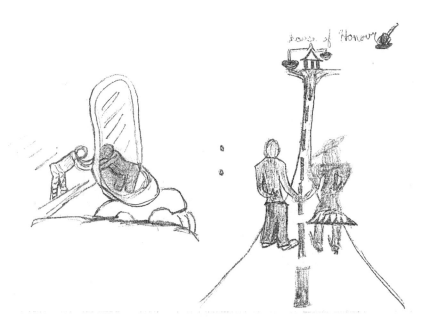

Please Illustrate or draw your own interpretation of the Scripture:

PROVERBS 4:8 Exalt her, and she shall promote thee: she shall bring thee to honour, when thou dost embrace her.

PROVERBS 5:14 I was almost in all evil in the midst of the congregation and assembly.

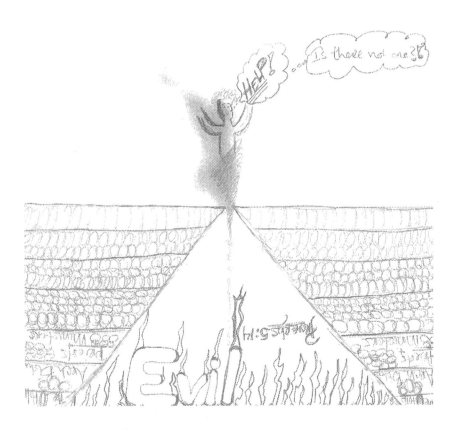

Please Illustrate or draw your own interpretation of the Scripture:

PROVERBS 5:14 I was almost in all evil in the midst of the congregation and assembly.

PROVERBS 6:15 Therefore shall his calamity come suddenly; suddenly shall he be broken without remedy.

+Now
+Before

+Right Now
+Right After

Please Illustrate or draw your own interpretation of the Scripture:

PROVERBS 6:15 Therefore shall his calamity come suddenly; suddenly shall he be broken without remedy.

PROVERBS 7:25 Let not thine heart decline
to her ways, go not astray in her paths.

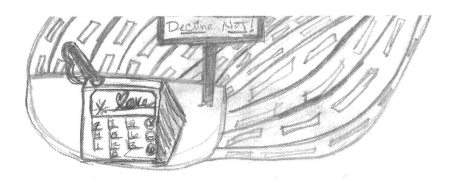

Please Illustrate or draw your own interpretation of the Scripture:

**PROVERBS 7:25 Let not thine heart decline
to her ways, go not astray in her paths.**

PROVERBS 8:21 That I may cause
those that love me to inherit substance;
and I will fill their treasures.

Please Illustrate or draw your own interpretation of the Scripture:

PROVERBS 8:21 That I may cause
those that love me to inherit substance;
and I will fill their treasures.

PROVERBS 9:8 Reprove not a scorner, lest he hate thee: rebuke a wise man, and he will love thee.

Please Illustrate or draw your own interpretation of the Scripture:

PROVERBS 9:8 Reprove not a scorner, lest he hate thee: rebuke a wise man, and he will love thee.

PROVERBS 10:11 The mouth of a righteous man is a well of life: but violence covereth the mouth of the wicked.

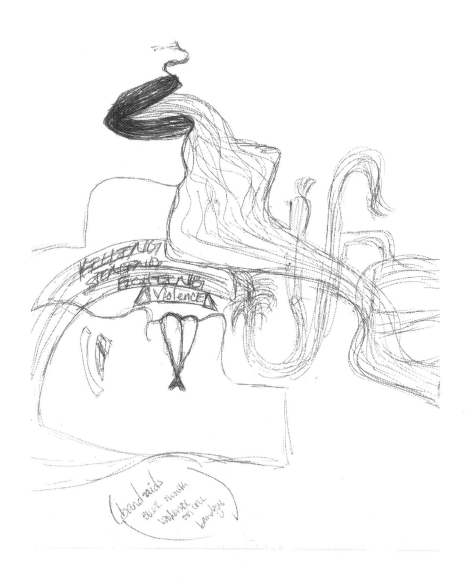

Please Illustrate or draw your own interpretation of the Scripture:

PROVERBS 10:11 The mouth of a
righteous man is a well of life: but violence
covereth the mouth of the wicked.

PROVERBS 11:1 false balance is abomination to the LORD: but a just weight is his delight.

22

Please Illustrate or draw your own interpretation of the Scripture:

PROVERBS 11:1 false balance is abomination to the LORD: but a just weight is his delight.

PROVERBS 12:3 A man shall not be
established by wickedness: but the root
of the righteous shall not be moved.

24

Please Illustrate or draw your own interpretation of the Scripture:

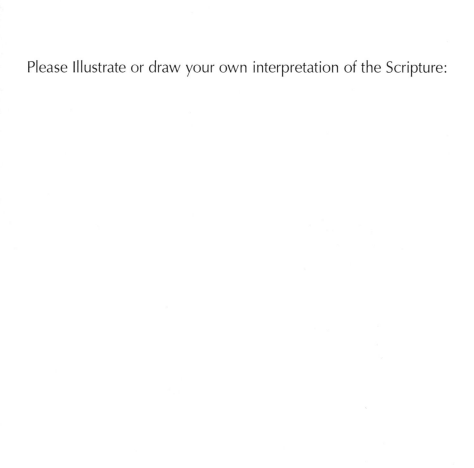

PROVERBS 12:3 A man shall not be established by wickedness: but the root of the righteous shall not be moved.

PROVERBS 13:3 He that keepeth his mouth keepeth his life: but he that openeth wide his lips shall have destruction.

Please Illustrate or draw your own interpretation of the Scripture:

PROVERBS 13:3 He that keepeth his
mouth keepeth his life: but he that openeth
wide his lips shall have destruction.

PROVERBS 14:30 A sound heart is the life of the flesh: but envy the rottenness of the bones.

Please Illustrate or draw your own interpretation of the Scripture:

PROVERBS 14:30 A sound heart is the life of the flesh: but envy the rottenness of the bones.

PROVERBS 15:3 The eyes of the LORD are in every place, beholding the evil and the good.

Please Illustrate or draw your own interpretation of the Scripture:

PROVERBS 15:3 The eyes of the LORD are in
every place, beholding the evil and the good.

PROVERBS 16:2 All the ways of a man are clean in his own eyes; but the LORD weigheth the spirits.

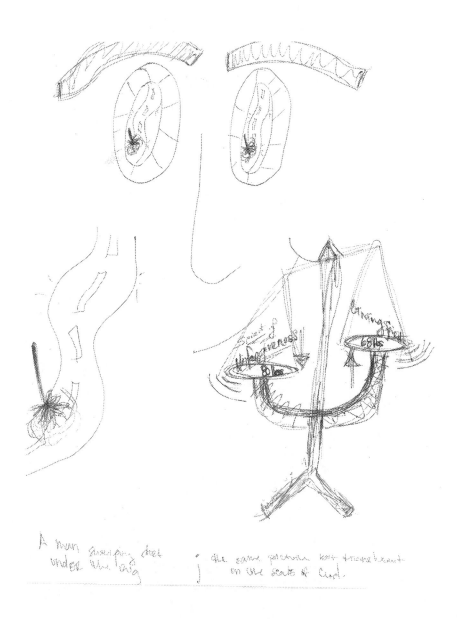

A man swaping dust under the rug

the same person but finds himself on the scales of God.

Please Illustrate or draw your own interpretation of the Scripture:

PROVERBS 16:2 All the ways of a man are clean in his own eyes; but the LORD weigheth the spirits.

PROVERBS 17:17 A friend loveth at all times, and a brother is born for adversity.

Please Illustrate or draw your own interpretation of the Scripture:

PROVERBS 17:17 A friend loveth at all times, and a brother is born for adversity.

PROVERBS 18:10 The name of the LORD is a strong tower: the righteous runneth into it, and is safe.

Please Illustrate or draw your own interpretation of the Scripture:

**PROVERBS 18:10 The name of the
LORD is a strong tower: the righteous
runneth into it, and is safe.**

PROVERBS 19:21 There are many devices in a man's heart; nevertheless the counsel of the LORD, that shall stand.

Please Illustrate or draw your own interpretation of the Scripture:

PROVERBS 19:21 There are many devices
in a man's heart; nevertheless the counsel
of the LORD, that shall stand.

PROVERBS 20:27 The spirit of man is the candle of the LORD, searching all the inward parts of the belly.

Please Illustrate or draw your own interpretation of the Scripture:

PROVERBS 20:27 The spirit of man
is the candle of the LORD, searching
all the inward parts of the belly.

PROVERBS 21:9 It is better to dwell in a corner of the housetop, than with a brawling woman in a wide house.

Please Illustrate or draw your own interpretation of the Scripture:

PROVERBS 21:9 It is better to dwell in
a corner of the housetop, than with a
brawling woman in a wide house.

PROVERBS 22:6 Train up a child in the way he should go: and when he is old, he will not depart from it.

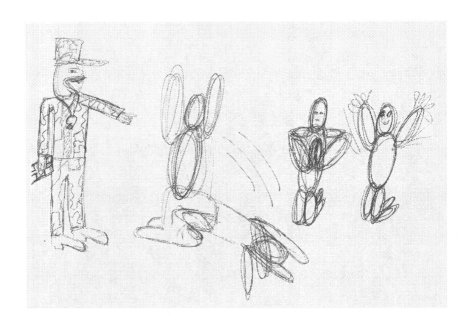

Please Illustrate or draw your own interpretation of the Scripture:

PROVERBS 22:6 Train up a child in the way he should go: and when he is old, he will not depart from it.

PROVERBS 23:17 Let not thine heart envy sinners: but be thou in the fear of the LORD all the day long.

Please Illustrate or draw your own interpretation of the Scripture:

PROVERBS 23:17 Let not thine heart envy sinners: but be thou in the fear of the LORD all the day long.

PROVERNS 24:16 For a just man falleth seven times, and riseth up again: but the wicked shall fall into mischief.

Please Illustrate or draw your own interpretation of the Scripture:

PROVERNS 24:16 For a just man falleth seven times, and riseth up again: but the wicked shall fall into mischief.

PROVERBS 25:11 A word fitly spoken is like apples of gold in pictures of silver.

Please Illustrate or draw your own interpretation of the Scripture:

PROVERBS 25:11 A word fitly spoken is like apples of gold in pictures of silver.

PROVERBS 26:11 As a dog returneth to his vomit, so a fool returneth to his folly.

Please Illustrate or draw your own interpretation of the Scripture:

PROVERBS 26:11 As a dog returneth to his vomit, so a fool returneth to his folly.

PROVERBS 27:1 Boast not thyself of to morrow; for thou knowest not what a day may bring forth.

Please Illustrate or draw your own interpretation of the Scripture:

PROVERBS 27:1 Boast not thyself of to morrow; for thou knowest not what a day may bring forth.

PROVERBS 28:1 The wicked flee when no man pursueth: but the righteous are bold as a lion.

Please Illustrate or draw your own interpretation of the Scripture:

PROVERBS 28:1 The wicked flee when no man pursueth: but the righteous are bold as a lion.

PROVERBS 29:2 When the righteous are in authority, the people rejoice: but when the wicked beareth rule, the people mourn.

Please Illustrate or draw your own interpretation of the Scripture:

PROVERBS 29:2 When the righteous are in authority, the people rejoice: but when the wicked beareth rule, the people mourn.

PROVERBS 30:33 Surely the churning of milk bringeth forth butter, and the wringing of the nose bringeth forth blood: so the forcing of wrath bringeth forth strife.

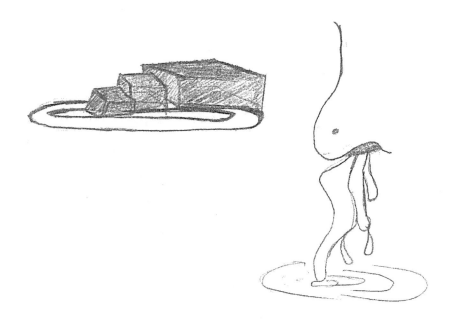

Please Illustrate or draw your own interpretation of the Scripture:

PROVERBS 30:33 Surely the churning of
milk bringeth forth butter, and the wringing
of the nose bringeth forth blood: so the
forcing of wrath bringeth forth strife.

PROVERBS 31:30 Favour is deceitful, and beauty is vain: but a woman that feareth the LORD, she shall be praised.

Please Illustrate or draw your own interpretation of the Scripture:

PROVERBS 31:30 Favour is deceitful, and beauty is vain: but a woman that feareth the LORD, she shall be praised.